ROME'S CHALLENGE

WHY DO PROTESTANTS KEEP SUNDAY?

A. T. JONES, EDITOR

 Adventist Pioneer Library

© 2018 Adventist Pioneer Library

37457 Jasper Lowell Rd
Jasper, OR, 97438, USA
+1 (877) 585-1111
www.APLib.org

These four articles were originally published in September 1893 by the *Catholic Mirror* and republished by A. T. Jones with additional comments in November 1893 as No. 15 of the *Religious Liberty Library*, International Religious Liberty Association, Battle Creek, Michigan. The only current update to these articles has been to remove abbreviations, add inserted definitions for archaic words, format long insertions, and make other minor editing.

Published in the USA

August, 2018

ISBN: 978-1-61455-062-4

TABLE OF CONTENTS

Why Do Protestants Keep Sunday? 5

The Christian Sabbath 7
   [From the *Catholic Mirror* of September 2, 1893.] 7
   [From the *Catholic Mirror* of September 9, 1893]. 12
   [From the *Catholic Mirror* of September 16, 1893.] 17
   [From the *Catholic Mirror* of September 23, 1893.] 24

Conclusion 29

Appendix 1 37

Appendix 2 41

WHY DO PROTESTANTS KEEP SUNDAY?

Most Christians assume that Sunday is the biblically approved day of worship. The Roman Catholic Church protests that it transferred Christian worship from the biblical Sabbath (Saturday) to Sunday, and that to try to argue that the change was made in the Bible is both dishonest and a denial of Catholic authority. If Protestantism wants to base its teachings only on the Bible, it should worship on Saturday.

February 24, 1893, the General Conference of Seventh day Adventists adopted certain resolutions appealing to the government and people of the United States regarding the decision of the Supreme Court declaring this to be a Christian nation, and regarding the action of Congress in legislating upon the subject of religion, and remonstrating against the principle and all the consequences of the same. In March, 1893, the International Religious Liberty Association printed these resolutions in a tract entitled *Appeal and Remonstrance*.

On receipt of one of these, the editor of the *Catholic Mirror* of Baltimore, Maryland, published a series of four editorials, which appeared in that paper September 2, 9, 16, and 23, 1893. The *Catholic Mirror* was the official organ of Cardinal Gibbons and the Papacy in the United States. These articles, therefore, although not written by the Cardinal's own hand, appeared under his official sanction, and as the expression of the Papacy on this subject, are the open challenge of the Papacy to Protestantism, and the demand of the Papacy that Protestants shall render to the Papacy an account of *why* they keep Sunday and also of *how* they keep it.

The following matter (excepting the footnotes, the editor's note in brackets signed "Editor," beginning on page 33 and ending on page 35, and the two Appendixes) is a verbatim reprint of these editorials, including the title on page 7.

THE PUBLISHERS

THE CHRISTIAN SABBATH

The Genuine Offspring of the Union of the Holy Spirit and the Catholic Church His Spouse. The Claims of Protestantism to Any Part Therein Proved to Be Groundless, Self-Contradictory, and Suicidal.

[From the *Catholic Mirror* of September 2, 1893.]

OUR attention has been called to the above subject in the past week by the receipt of a brochure of twenty-one pages, published by the International Religious Liberty Association, entitled, "Appeal and Remonstrance," embodying resolutions adopted by the General Conference of the Seventh-day Adventists (February 24, 1893). The resolutions criticize and censure, with much acerbity, the action of the United States Congress, and of the Supreme Court, for invading the rights of the people by closing the World's Fair on Sunday.

The Adventists are the only body of Christians with the Bible as their teacher, who can find no warrant in its pages for the change of day from the seventh to the first. Hence their appellation, "Seventh-day Adventists". Their cardinal principle consists in setting apart Saturday for the exclusive worship of God, in conformity with the positive command of God Himself, repeatedly reiterated in the sacred books of the Old and New Testaments, literally obeyed by the children of Israel for thousands of years to this day, and endorsed by the teaching and practice of the Son of God whilst on earth.

Per contra, the Protestants of the world, the Adventists excepted, with the *same* Bible as their cherished and sole infallible teacher, by their practice, since their appearance in the sixteenth century, with the time-honored practice of the Jewish people before their eyes, have rejected the day named for His worship by God, and assumed, in apparent contradiction of His command, a day for His worship never once referred to for that purpose, in the pages of that Sacred Volume.

What Protestant pulpit does not ring almost every Sunday with loud and impassioned invectives against Sabbath violation? Who can forget the fanatical clamor of the Protestant ministers throughout the length and breadth of the land against opening the gates of the World's Fair on Sunday? The thousands of petitions, signed by millions, to save the Lord's Day from desecration? Surely, such general and widespread excitement and noisy remonstrance could not have existed without the strongest grounds for such animated protests.

And when quarters were assigned at the World's Fair to the various sects of Protestantism for the exhibition of articles, who can forget the emphatic expression of virtuous and conscientious indignation exhibited by our Presbyterian brethren, as soon as they learned of the decision of the Supreme Court not to interfere in the Sunday opening? The newspapers informed us that they flatly refused to utilize the space accorded them, or open their boxes, demanding the right to withdraw the articles, in rigid adherence to their principles, and thus decline all contact with the sacrilegious and Sabbath-breaking Exhibition.

Doubtless, our Calvinistic brethren deserved and shared the sympathy of all the other sects, who, however, lost the opportunity of posing as martyrs in vindication of the Sabbath observance.

They thus became "a spectacle to the world, to angels, and to men," although their Protestant brethren, who failed to share the monopoly, were uncharitably and enviously disposed to attribute their steadfast adherence to religious principle, to Pharisaical pride and dogged obstinacy.

Our purpose in throwing off this article, is to shed such light on this all-important question (for were the Sabbath question to be removed from the Protestant pulpit, the sects would feel lost, and the preachers be deprived of their "Cheshire cheese") that our readers may be able to comprehend the question in *all its bearings*, and thus reach a clear conviction.

The Christian world is, morally speaking, united on the question and practice of worshiping God on *the first day* of the week.

The Israelites, scattered all over the earth, keep *the last day* of the week sacred to the worship of the Deity. In this particular, the Seventh-day Adventists (a sect of Christians numerically few) have also selected the same day.

The Israelites and Adventists both appeal to the Bible for the divine command, persistently obliging the strict observance of Saturday.

The Israelite respects the authority of the Old Testament only, but the Adventist, who is a Christian, accepts the New Testament on the same ground as the Old: viz., an inspired record also. He finds that the Bible, his teacher, is consistent in both parts, that the Redeemer, during His mortal life, never kept any other day than Saturday. The Gospels plainly evince to him this fact; whilst, in the pages of the Acts of the Apostles, the Epistles, and the Apocalypse, not the vestige of an act canceling the Saturday arrangement can be found.

The Adventists, therefore, in common with the Israelites, derive their belief from the Old Testament, which position is confirmed by the New Testament, endorsing fully by the life and practice of the Redeemer and His apostles the teaching of the Sacred Word for nearly a century of the Christian era.

Numerically considered, the Seventh-day Adventists form an insignificant portion of the Protestant population of the earth, but, as the question is not one of numbers, but of truth, fact, and right, a strict sense of justice forbids the condemnation of this little sect without a calm and unbiased investigation;[1] this is none of our funeral.

The Protestant world has been, from its infancy, in the sixteenth century, in thorough accord with the Catholic Church, in keeping "holy," not Saturday, but Sunday. The discussion of the grounds that led to this unanimity of sentiment and practice for over 300 years, must help toward placing Protestantism on a solid basis in this particular, should the arguments in favor of its position overcome those furnished by the Israelites and Adventists, the Bible, the sole recognized teacher of both litigants, being the umpire and witness. If, however, on the other hand, the latter furnish arguments, incontrovertible by the great mass of Protestants, both classes of litigants, appealing to their common teacher, the Bible, the great body of Protestants, so far from clamoring, as they do with vigorous pertinacity for the strict keeping of Sunday, have no other recourse left than the admission that they have been teaching and practicing *what is Scripturally false for over three centuries*, by adopting the teaching and practice of what they have always pretended to believe an apostate church, contrary to every warrant and teaching of sacred Scripture. To add to the intensity of this Scriptural and unpardonable blunder, it involves one of the most positive and

---

[1] Is this a hint that the investigation and consequent condemnation of the Seventh-day Adventists will be dully carried into effect by Rome, as soon as this "calm and unbiased investigation," shall have been completed with the Protestants with whom she is now dealing? — Editor.

emphatic commands of God to His servant, man: "Remember the Sabbath day, to keep it holy."

No Protestant living today has ever yet obeyed that command, preferring to follow the apostate church referred to than his teacher, the Bible, which, from Genesis to Revelation, *teaches no other doctrine*, should the Israelites and Seventh-day Adventists be correct. Both sides appeal to the Bible as their "infallible" teacher. Let the Bible decide whether Saturday or Sunday be the day enjoined by God. One of the two bodies must be wrong, and, whereas a false position on this all-important question involves terrible penalties, threatened by God Himself, against the transgressor of this "perpetual covenant," we shall enter on the discussion of the merits of the arguments wielded by both sides. Neither is the discussion of this paramount subject above the capacity of ordinary minds, nor does it involve extraordinary study. It resolves itself into a few plain questions easy of solution:

1st. Which day of the week does the Bible enjoin to be kept holy?

2nd. Has the New Testament modified by precept or practice the original command?

3rd. Have Protestants, since the sixteenth century, obeyed the command of God by keeping "holy" the day enjoined by their infallible guide and teacher, the Bible? and if not, why not?

To the above three questions we pledge ourselves to furnish as many intelligent answers, which cannot fail to vindicate the truth and uphold the deformity of error.

[From the *Catholic Mirror* of September 9, 1893]

> "But faith, fanatic faith, once wedded fast
> To some dear falsehood, hugs it to the last."
>
> — Moore.

Conformably to our promise in our last issue, we proceed to unmask one of the most flagrant errors and most unpardonable inconsistencies of the Biblical rule of faith. Lest, however, we be misunderstood, we deem it necessary to premise that Protestantism recognizes no rule of faith, no teacher, save the "infallible Bible." As the Catholic yields his judgment in spiritual matters implicitly, and with unreserved confidence, to the voice of his church, so, too, the Protestant recognizes *no teacher but the Bible*. All his spirituality is derived from its teachings. It is to him the voice of God addressing him through his sole inspired teacher. It embodies his religion, his faith, and his practice. The language of Chillingworth, "The Bible, the whole Bible, and nothing but the Bible, is the religion of Protestants," is only one form of the same idea multifariously convertible into other forms, such as "the Book of God," "the Charter of Our Salvation," "the Oracle of Our Christian Faith," "God's Text-Book to the race of Mankind," etc., etc. It is, then, an incontrovertible fact that *the Bible alone* is the teacher of Protestant Christianity. Assuming this fact, we will now proceed to discuss the merits of the question involved in our last issue.

Recognizing what is undeniable, the fact of a direct contradiction between the teaching and practice of Protestant Christianity — the Seventh-day Adventists excepted — on the one hand, and that of the Jewish people on the other, both observing different days of the week for the worship of God, we will proceed to take the testimony of the only available witness in the premises: viz., the testimony of the teacher common to both claimants, the Bible. The first expression with which we come in contact in the Sacred Word, is found in Genesis 2:2: "And on the seventh day He [God] rested from all His work which He had made." The next reference to this matter is to be found in Exodus 20, where God commanded the seventh day to be kept, *because* He had Himself rested from the work of creation on that day; and the sacred text informs us that *for that reason* He desired it kept, in the following words: "*Wherefore*, the Lord blessed the seventh day and sanctified it."[2] Again, we read in chapter 31, verse 15: "Six days you shall do work; in the seventh day is the Sabbath, the rest holy to the Lord;" sixteenth verse: "*It is an everlasting covenant*," "and a perpetual sign," "for in six days the Lord made heaven and earth, and in the seventh He ceased from work."

In the Old Testament, reference is made one hundred and twenty-six times to the Sabbath, and all these texts conspire harmoniously in voicing the will of God commanding the seventh day to be kept, because God Himself *first kept it*, making it obligatory on all as *"a perpetual covenant."* Nor can we imagine any one foolhardy enough to question the identity of Saturday with the Sabbath or seventh day, seeing that the people of Israel have been keeping the Saturday from the giving of the law, A. M. 2514 to A. D. 1893, a period of 3383 years. With the example of the Israelites before our eyes today, there is no historical fact better established than that referred to; viz., that the chosen people of God, the guardians of the Old Testament, the living representatives of the only divine religion hitherto, had for a period of 1490 years anterior to Christianity, preserved by weekly

---

[2] Of course the scriptures quoted throughout in these editorials are from the Douay, or Catholic, Version. — Editor.

practice the living tradition of the correct interpretation of the special day of the week, Saturday, to be kept "holy to the Lord," which tradition they have extended by their practice to an additional period of 1893 years more, thus covering the full extent of the Christian dispensation. We deem it necessary to be perfectly clear on this point, for reasons that will appear more fully hereafter. The Bible — the Old Testament — confirmed by the living tradition of a weekly practice for 3383 years by the chosen people of God, teaches, then, with absolute certainty, that God had, Himself, named the day to be "kept holy to Him," — that the day was Saturday, and that any violation of that command was punishable with death. "Keep you My Sabbath, for it is holy unto you; he that shall profane it shall be put to death; he that shall do any work in it, his soul shall perish in the midst of his people." Exodus 31:14.

It is impossible to realize a more severe penalty than that so solemnly uttered by God Himself in the above text, on all who violate a command referred to no less than one hundred and twenty-six times in the old law. The ten commandments of the Old Testament are formally impressed on the memory of the child of the Biblical Christian as soon as possible, but there is not one of the ten made more emphatically familiar, both in Sunday school and pulpit, than that of keeping "holy" the Sabbath day.

Having secured with absolute certainty the will of God as regards the day to be kept holy, from His Sacred Word, *because* He rested on that day, which day is confirmed to us by the practice of His chosen people for thousands of years, we are naturally induced to inquire *when and where* God changed the day for His worship; for it is patent to the world that a change of day has taken place, and inasmuch as no indication of such change can be found within the pages of the Old Testament, nor in the practice of the Jewish people who continue for nearly nineteen centuries of Christianity obeying the written command, we must look to the exponent of the Christian dispensation; viz., the New Testament, for the command of God canceling the old Sabbath, Saturday.

We now approach a period covering little short of nineteen centuries, and proceed to investigate whether the supplemental divine teacher — the New Testament — contains a decree canceling the mandate of the old law, and, at the same time, substituting a day for the divinely instituted Sabbath of the old law, viz. Saturday; for, inasmuch as Saturday was the day kept and ordered to be kept by God, *divine authority alone*, under the form of a canceling decree, could abolish the Saturday covenant, and another divine mandate, appointing by name another day to be kept "holy," other than Saturday, is equally necessary to satisfy the conscience of the Christian believer. The Bible being the only teacher recognized by the Biblical Christian, the Old Testament failing to point out a change of day, and yet another day than Saturday being kept "holy" by the Biblical world, it is surely incumbent on the reformed Christian to point out in the pages of the New Testament the new divine decree repealing that of Saturday and substituting that of Sunday, kept by Biblicals since the dawn of the Reformation.

Examining the New Testament from cover to cover, critically, we find the Sabbath referred to sixty-one times. We find, too, that the Saviour invariably selected the Sabbath (Saturday) to teach in the synagogues and work miracles. The four Gospels refer to the Sabbath (Saturday) fifty-one times.

In one instance the Redeemer refers to Himself as "the Lord of the Sabbath," as mentioned by Matthew and Luke,[3] but during the whole record of His life, whilst invariably keeping and utilizing the day (Saturday), *He never once hinted at a*

---

[3] It is also referred to in Mark 2:28. — Editor.

desire to change it. His apostles and personal friends afford to us a striking instance of their scrupulous observance of it *after His death*, and, whilst His body was yet in the tomb, Luke (23:56) informs us: "And they returned and prepared spices and ointments, *and rested on the Sabbath day according to the commandment.*" "But on the first day of the week, very early in the morning, they came, bringing the spices they had prepared." The "spices" and "ointments" had been prepared Good Friday evening, because the "Sabbath drew near." Verse 54. This action on the part of the personal friends of the Saviour, proves beyond contradiction that *after His death* they kept "holy" the Saturday, *and regarded the Sunday as any other day of the week.* Can anything, therefore, be more conclusive than that the apostles and the holy women never knew any Sabbath but Saturday, up to the day of Christ's death?

We now approach the investigation of this interesting question for the next thirty years, as narrated by the evangelist, St. Luke, in his Acts of the Apostles. Surely some vestige of the canceling act can be discovered in the practice of the apostles during that protracted period.

But, alas! We are once more doomed to disappointment. *Nine times* do we find the Sabbath referred to in the Acts, but it is the *Saturday* (the old Sabbath). Should our readers desire the proof, we refer them to chapter and verse in each instance. Acts 1:12; 13:14, 27, 42, 44. Once more, Acts 15:21; again, Acts 16:13; 17:2; 18:4. "And he (Paul) reasoned in the synagogue *every Sabbath*, and persuaded the Jews and the Greeks." *Thus the Sabbath (Saturday) from Genesis to Revelation!!!* Thus, it is impossible to find in the New Testament the slightest interference by the Saviour or His apostles with the original Sabbath, but on the contrary, an entire acquiescence in the original arrangement; nay, a *plenary endorsement* by Him, whilst living; and an unvaried, active participation *in the keeping of that day and no other by the apostles,* for thirty years after His death, as the Acts of the Apostles has abundantly testified to us.

Hence the conclusion is inevitable; viz., that of those who follow the Bible as their guide, the Israelites and Seventh-day Adventists have the exclusive weight of evidence on their side, whilst the Biblical Protestant has not a word in self-defense for his substitution of Sunday for Saturday. More anon.

[From the *Catholic Mirror* of September 16, 1893.]

When his satanic majesty, who was "a murderer from the beginning," "and the father of lies," undertook to open the eyes of our first mother, Eve, by stimulating her ambition, "You shall be as gods, knowing good and evil," his action was but the first of many plausible and successful efforts employed later, in the seduction of millions of her children. Like Eve, they learn too late, alas! the value of the inducements held out to allure her weak children from allegiance to God. Nor does the subject matter of this discussion form an exception to the usual tactics of his sable majesty.

Over three centuries since, he plausibly represented to a large number of discontented and ambitious Christians the bright prospect of the successful inauguration of a "new departure," by the abandonment of the Church instituted by the Son of God, as their teacher, and the assumption of a new teacher — *the Bible alone* — as their newly fledged oracle.

The sagacity of the evil one foresaw but the brilliant success of this maneuver. Nor did the result fall short of his most sanguine expectations.

A bold and adventurous spirit was alone needed to head the expedition. His satanic majesty soon found in the apostate monk, Luther, who himself repeatedly testifies to the close familiarity that existed between his master and himself, in his "Table Talk," and other works published in 1558, at Wittenberg, under the inspection of Melancthon. His colloquies with Satan on various occasions, are testified to by Luther himself — a witness worthy of all credibility. What the agency of the serpent tended so effectually to achieve in the garden, the agency of Luther achieved in the Christian world.[4]

> *"Give them a pilot to their wandering fleet,*
> *Bold in his art, and tutored to deceit;*
> *Whose hand adventurous shall their helm misguide*
> *To hostile shores, or 'whelm them in the tide."*

As the end proposed to himself by the Evil One in his raid on the Church of Christ was the destruction of Christianity, we are now engaged in sifting the means adopted by him to insure his success therein. So far, they have been found to be misleading, self-contradictory, and fallacious. We will now proceed with the further investigation of this imposture.

Having proved to a demonstration that the Redeemer, *in no instance*, had, during the period of His life, deviated from the faithful observance of the Sabbath (Saturday), referred to

---

[4] Of course we have not the least sympathy with what is here said about Luther. Only the Lutherans think that Luther had all the truth, but his was nevertheless a grand work. He was a Christian hero. Had his work been only continued as it began, papists would not now be taunting "Protestants" with the inconsistency of professing to accept the Bible alone and then following the traditions of the Catholic Church. — Editor.

The Christian Sabbath

by the four evangelists fifty-one times, although He had designated Himself "Lord of the Sabbath," He never having *once*, by command or practice, hinted at a desire on His part to change the day by the substitution of another and having called special attention to the conduct of the apostles and the holy women, the very evening of His death, securing beforehand spices and ointments to be used in embalming His body the morning after the Sabbath (Saturday), as St. Luke so clearly informs us (Luke 24:1), thereby placing beyond peradventure, the divine action and will of the Son of God during life by keeping the Sabbath steadfastly; and having called attention to the action of His living representatives after His death, as proved by St. Luke; having also placed before our readers *the indisputable fact* that the apostles for the following thirty years (Acts) never deviated from the practice of their divine Master in this particular, as St. Luke (Acts 18:4) assures us: "And he [Paul] reasoned in the synagogues *every Sabbath* (Saturday), and persuaded the Jews and the Greeks." The Gentile converts were, as we see from the text, equally instructed with the Jews, to keep the Saturday, having been converted to Christianity on that day, "the Jews and the Greeks" collectively.

Having also called attention to the nine texts of the Acts bearing on the exclusive use of the Sabbath by the Jews and Christians for thirty years after the death of the Saviour as the *only* day of the week observed by Christ and His apostles, which period *exhausts the inspired record*, we now proceed to supplement our proofs that the Sabbath (Saturday) enjoyed this exclusive privilege, by calling attention to *every instance* wherein the sacred record refers to the first day of the week.

The *first* reference to Sunday after the resurrection of Christ is to be found in St. Luke's Gospel, chapter 24, verses 33-40, and St. John 20:19.

The above texts themselves refer to the sole motive of this gathering on the part of the apostles. It took place on the day of the resurrection (Easter Sunday), not for the purpose of inaugurating "the new departure" from the old Sabbath (Saturday) by keeping "holy" the new day, for there is not a hint given of prayer, exhortation, or the reading of the Scriptures, but it indicates the utter demoralization of the apostles by informing mankind that they were huddled together in that room in Jerusalem *"for fear of the Jews,"* as St. John, quoted above, plainly informs us.

The second reference to Sunday is to be found in St. John's Gospel, 20th chapter, 26th to 29th verses: "And after eight days, the disciples were again within, and Thomas with them."[5] The resurrected Redeemer availed Himself of this meeting of all the apostles to confound the incredulity of Thomas, who had been absent from the gathering on Easter Sunday evening. This would have furnished a golden opportunity to the Redeemer to change the day in the presence of all His apostles, but we state the simple fact that, on this occasion, as on Easter day, not a word is said of prayer, praise, or reading of the Scriptures.

The third instance on record, wherein the apostles were assembled on Sunday, is to be found in Acts 2:1; "The apostles were all of one accord in one place." (Feast of Pentecost — Sunday.)[6] Now, will this text afford to our Biblical Christian brethren a vestige of hope that Sunday substitutes, at length, Saturday?

---

[5] It is a "Protestant" claim that this passage refers to Sunday. The *Mirror* not only notices it, but admits the correctness of the claim. But how anybody can find in this text a reference to Sunday or the first day of the week, is a mystery. The previous meeting was on the first day of the week: the word says so. From this to the next first day of the week would be just one week. Now in one week there are just *seven* days and no more. But the Sacred Word says that this meeting was *after* EIGHT days. How anybody can get more than eight days into a week is a mystery of numbers and of the calendar, to say nothing of its confusion of the Sacred Word, that is bewildering to plain minds. However, this mystery is no greater nor any more bewildering than that by which Sunday has been substituted for the Sabbath of the Lord. — Editor.

[6] Pentecost was not on Sunday. See next note. — Editor.

For when we inform them that the Jews had been keeping *this Sunday* for 1500 years, and have been keeping it for eighteen centuries after the establishment of Christianity, at the same time keeping the weekly Sabbath, there is not to be found either consolation or comfort in this text. Pentecost is the fiftieth day after the Passover,[7] which was called the Sabbath of weeks, consisting of seven times seven days; and the day after the completion of the seventh weekly Sabbath day, was the chief day of the entire festival, necessarily Sunday. What Israelite would not pity the cause that would seek to discover the origin of the keeping of the first day of the week in his festival of Pentecost, that has been kept by him yearly for over 3,000 years? Who but the Biblical Christian, driven to the wall for a pretext to excuse his sacrilegious desecration of the Sabbath, always kept by Christ and His apostles, would have resorted to the Jewish festival of Pentecost for his act of rebellion against his God and his teacher, the Bible?

Once more, the Biblical apologists for the change of day call our attention to the Acts, chapter 20, verses 6 and 7: "And upon *the first day of the week*, when the disciples came together

---

[7] Our Saviour ate the Passover with His disciples the night before His crucifixion, and He was crucified on Friday. Friday, therefore, was the first day of the feast of the Passover, or of unleavened bread. The morrow after that day was the day from which the fifty days to Pentecost were to be counted. Leviticus 23:6, 11, 15, 16. The morrow after that day being "the Sabbath day according to the commandment" (Luke 23:56), and the first day of the fifty, it is evident that the fiftieth day itself would be not Sunday but Saturday. Anybody can demonstrate this for himself who will begin with "the morrow after" any Friday and count fifty. And as the Passover was always the fourteenth day of the first *month*, without any reference whatever to any particular day of the *week*, it were impossible that the Pentecost should always be "necessarily Sunday," as stated. Of course this note, true though it be, has no bearing upon this question as between Catholics and Protestants, as both claim — the Catholics originally — that this particular Pentecost was on Sunday. This note is inserted merely in the interests of accuracy, and not with the intention that it should have any bearing on the controversy in the text. — Editor.

to break bread," etc. To all appearances, the above text should furnish some consolation to our disgruntled Biblical friends, but being a Marplot [or meddler], we cannot allow them even this crumb of comfort. We reply by the axiom: "*Quod probat nimis, probat nihil*" — "What proves too much, proves nothing." Let us call attention to the same, Acts 2:46: "And they, continuing *daily* in the temple, and breaking bread from house to house," etc. Who does not see at a glance that the text produced to prove the exclusive prerogative of Sunday, vanishes into thin air — an *ignis fatuus* — when placed in juxtaposition with the 46th verse of the same chapter? What the Biblical Christian claims by this text *for Sunday alone* the same authority, St. Luke, informs us was *common to every day of the week:* "And they, continuing *daily* in the temple, and breaking bread from house to house."

One text more presents itself, apparently leaning toward a substitution of Sunday for Saturday. It is taken from St. Paul, 1 Corinthians 16:1, 2: "Now concerning the collection for the saints." "On the first day of the week, let every one of you lay by him in store," etc. Presuming that the request of St. Paul had been strictly attended to, let us call attention to what had been done each Saturday during the Saviour's life and continued for thirty years after, as the book of Acts informs us.

The followers of the Master met "*every Sabbath*" to hear the word of God; the Scriptures were read "*every Sabbath day.*" "And Paul, as his manner was to reason in the synagogue *every Sabbath*, interposing the name of the Lord Jesus," etc. Acts 18:4. What more absurd conclusion than to infer that reading of the Scriptures, prayer, exhortation, and preaching, which *formed the routine duties of every Saturday*, as has been abundantly proved, were overslaughed by a request to take up a collection on *another day of the week*?

In order to appreciate fully the value of this text now under consideration, it is only needful to recall the action of the apostles and holy women on Good Friday before sundown. They brought the spices and ointments after He was taken down from the cross; they suspended all action until the Sabbath "holy to the Lord" had passed, and then took steps on Sunday morning to complete the process of embalming the sacred body of Jesus.

Why, may we ask, did they not proceed to complete the work of embalming on Saturday? — Because they knew well that the embalming of the sacred body of their Master would interfere with the strict observance of the Sabbath, the keeping of which was paramount; and until it can be shown that the Sabbath day *immediately preceding the Sunday of our text* had not been kept (which would be false, inasmuch as *every Sabbath had been kept*), the request of St. Paul to make the collection *on Sunday* remains to be classified with the work of the embalming of Christ's body, which could not be effected on the Sabbath, and was consequently deferred to the next convenient day; viz., Sunday, or the first day of the week.

Having disposed of every text to be found in the New Testament referring to the Sabbath (Saturday), and to the first day of the week (Sunday); and having shown conclusively from these texts, that, so far, not a shadow of pretext can be found in the Sacred Volume for the Biblical substitution of Sunday for Saturday; it only remains for us to investigate the meaning of the expressions "Lord's Day," and "day of the Lord," to be found in the New Testament, which we propose to do in our next article, and conclude with apposite remarks on the incongruities of a system of religion which we shall have proved to be indefensible, self-contradictory, and suicidal.

[From the *Catholic Mirror* of September 23, 1893.]

> "Halting on crutches of unequal size,
> One leg by truth supported, *one by lies*,
> Thus sidle to the goal with awkward pace,
> *Secure of nothing but to lose the race.*"

In the present article we propose to investigate carefully a new (and the last) class of proof assumed to convince the Biblical Christian that God had substituted Sunday for Saturday for His worship in the new law, and that the divine will is to be found recorded by the Holy Ghost in apostolic writings.

We are informed that this radical change has found expression, over and over again, in a series of texts in which the expression, "the day of the Lord," or "the Lord's day," is to be found.

The class of texts in the New Testament, under the title "Sabbath," numbering sixty-one in the Gospels, Acts, and Epistles; and the second class, in which "the first day of the week," or Sunday, having been critically examined (the latter class numbering nine [eight]); and having been found not to afford the slightest clue to a change of will on the part of God as to His day of worship by man, we now proceed to examine the third and last class of texts relied on to save the Biblical system from the arraignment of seeking to palm off on the world, in the name of God, a decree for which there is not the slightest warrant or authority from their teacher, the Bible.

The first text of this class is to be found in the Acts of the Apostles, 2:20: "The sun shall be turned into darkness, and the moon into blood, before that great and notable *day of the Lord* shall come." How many Sundays have rolled by since that prophecy was spoken? So much for that effort to pervert the meaning of the sacred text from the judgment day to Sunday!

The second text of this class is to be found in 1 Corinthians 1:8: "Who shall also confirm you unto the end, that you may be blameless *in the day of our Lord Jesus Christ.*" What simpleton does not see that the apostle here plainly indicates the day of judgment? The next text of this class that presents itself is to be found in the same Epistle, chapter 5:5: "To deliver such a one to Satan for the destruction of the flesh, that the spirit may be saved *in the day of the Lord Jesus.*" The incestuous Corinthian was, of course, saved on the *Sunday next following!!* How pitiable such a makeshift as this! The fourth text, 2 Corinthians 1:13, 14: "And I trust ye shall acknowledge even to the end, even as ye also are ours in the day of our Lord Jesus."

Sunday, or the day of judgment, which? The fifth text is from St. Paul to the Philippians, chapter 1, verse 6: "Being confident of this very thing, that He who hath begun a good work in you, will perfect it *until the day of Jesus Christ.*" The good people of Philippi, in attaining perfection *on the following Sunday*, could afford to laugh at our modern rapid transit!

We beg leave to submit our sixth of the class; viz., Philippians, first chapter, tenth verse: "That he may be sincere without offense unto *the day of Christ.*" That day was *next Sunday*, forsooth! not so long to wait after all. The seventh text, 2 Peter 3:10: "But *the day of the Lord* will come as a thief in the night." The application of this text to Sunday passes the bounds of absurdity.

The eighth text, 2 Peter 3:12: "Waiting for and hastening unto *the coming of the day of the Lord*, by which the heavens being on fire, shall be dissolved," etc. This day of the Lord is the same referred to in the previous text, the application of both of which *to Sunday next* would have left the Christian world sleepless the next Saturday night.

We have presented to our readers eight of the nine texts relied on to bolster up by text of Scripture the sacrilegious effort to palm off the "Lord's day" for Sunday, and with what result? Each furnishes *prima facie* evidence of the last day, referring to it directly, absolutely, and unequivocally.

The ninth text wherein we meet the expression "the Lord's day," is the last to be found in the apostolic writings. The Apocalypse, or Revelation, chapter 1:10, furnishes it in the following words of St. John: "I was in the Spirit on the Lord's day;" but it will afford no more comfort to our Biblical friends than its predecessors of the same series. Has St. John used the expression previously in his Gospel or Epistles? — Emphatically, *No*. Has he had occasion to refer to Sunday hitherto? — Yes, twice. How did he designate Sunday on these occasions? Easter Sunday was called by him (John 20:1) *"the first day of the week."*

Again, chapter twenty, nineteenth verse: "Now when it was late that same day, *being the first day of the week.*" Evidently, although inspired, both in his Gospel and Epistles, he called Sunday "the first day of the week." On what grounds, then, can it be assumed that he dropped that designation? Was he *more inspired* when he wrote the Apocalypse, or did he adopt a new title for Sunday, because it was now in vogue?

A reply to these questions would be supererogatory especially to the latter, seeing that the same expression had been used eight times already by St. Luke, St. Paul, and St. Peter, *all under divine inspiration*, and surely the Holy Spirit would not inspire St. John to call Sunday the Lord's day, whilst He inspired Sts. Luke, Paul, and Peter, collectively, to entitle the day of judgment "the Lord's day." Dialecticians reckon amongst the infallible motives of certitude, the moral motive of analogy or induction, by which we are enabled to conclude with certainty from the known to the unknown; being absolutely certain of the meaning of an expression uttered eight times, we conclude that the same expression can have only the same meaning when uttered the ninth time, especially when we know that on the nine occasions the expressions were *inspired by the Holy Spirit*.

Nor are the strongest intrinsic grounds wanting to prove that this, like its sister texts, contains the same meaning. St. John (Revelation 1:10) says: "I was in the Spirit on the Lord's day;" but he furnishes us the key to this expression, chapter four, first and second verses. "After this I looked and behold a door was opened in heaven." A voice said to him: "Come up hither, and I will show you *the things which must be hereafter*." Let us ascend in spirit with John. Whither? — through that "door in heaven," to heaven. And what shall we see? — "The things that must be hereafter," chapter four, first verse. He ascended in spirit to heaven. He was ordered to write, in full, his vision of what is to take place antecedent to, and concomitantly with, "the Lord's day," or the day of Judgment; the expression "Lord's day" being confined in Scripture to the day of Judgment exclusively.

We have studiously and accurately collected from the New Testament every available proof that could be adduced in favor of a law canceling the Sabbath day of the old law, or one substituting another day for the Christian dispensation. We have been careful to make the above distinction, lest it might be advanced that the third[8] commandment was abrogated under the new law. Any such plea has been overruled by the action of the Methodist Episcopal bishops in their pastoral 1874, and quoted by the New York *Herald* of the same date, of the following tenor: "The Sabbath instituted in the beginning and confirmed again and again by Moses and the prophets, *has never been abrogated*. A part of the moral law, not a part or tittle of its sanctity has been taken away." The above official pronunciamento has committed

---

[8] In the Catholic enumeration, the fourth — the Sabbath — commandment is the *third* of the ten commandments. — Editor.

that large body of Biblical Christians to the permanence of the third commandment under the new law.

We again beg leave to call the special attention of our readers to the twentieth of "the thirty-nine articles of religion" of the Book of Common Prayer: "It is not lawful for the church to ordain anything that is contrary to *God's written word.*"

Conclusion

We have in this series of articles, taken much pains for the instruction of our readers to prepare them by presenting a number of *undeniable facts* found in the word of God, to arrive at a conclusion absolutely irrefragable. When the Biblical system put in an appearance in the sixteenth century, it not only seized on the temporal possessions of the Church, but in its vandalic crusade stripped Christianity, as far as it could, of all the sacraments instituted by its Founder, of the holy sacrifice, etc., etc., retaining nothing but the Bible, which its exponents pronounced *their sole teacher* in Christian doctrine and morals.

Chief amongst their articles of belief was, and is today, the permanent necessity of keeping the Sabbath holy. In fact, it has been for the past 300 years the only article of the Christian belief in which there has been a plenary consensus of Biblical representatives. The keeping of the Sabbath constitutes the sum and substance of the Biblical theory. The pulpits resound weekly with incessant tirades against the lax manner of keeping the Sabbath in Catholic countries, as contrasted with the proper, Christian, self-satisfied mode of keeping the day in Biblical countries. Who can ever forget the virtuous indignation manifested by the Biblical preachers throughout the length and breadth of our country, from every Protestant pulpit, as long as the question of opening the World's Fair on Sunday was yet undecided; and who does not know today, that one sect, to mark its holy indignation at the decision, has never yet opened the boxes that contained its articles at the World's Fair?

These superlatively good and unctuous Christians, by conning over their Bible carefully, can find their counterpart in a certain class of remarkably good people in the days of the Redeemer, who haunted Him night and day, distressed beyond measure, and scandalized beyond forbearance, because He did not keep the Sabbath in as straight-laced manner as themselves.

They hated Him for using common sense in reference to the day, and He found no epithets expressive enough of His supreme contempt for their Pharisaical pride. And it is very probable that the divine mind has not modified its views today concerning the blatant outcry of their followers and sympathizers at the close of this nineteenth century. But when we add to all this the fact that whilst the Pharisees of old kept the *true Sabbath*, our modern Pharisees, counting on the credulity and simplicity of their dupes, *have never once in their lives kept the true Sabbath* which their divine Master kept to His dying day, and which His apostles kept, after His example, for thirty years afterward, according to the Sacred Record, the most glaring contradiction, involving a deliberate sacrilegious rejection of a most positive precept is presented to us today in the action of the Biblical Christian world. The Bible and the Sabbath constitute the watchword of Protestantism; but we have demonstrated that it is *the Bible against their Sabbath*. We have shown that no greater contradiction ever existed than their theory and practice. We have proved that neither their Biblical ancestors nor themselves have ever kept one Sabbath day in their lives.

The Israelites and Seventh-day Adventists are witnesses of their weekly desecration of the day named by God so repeatedly, and whilst they have ignored and condemned their teacher, the Bible, they have adopted a day kept by the Catholic Church. What Protestant can, after perusing these articles, with a clear conscience, continue to disobey the command of God, enjoining *Saturday to be kept*, which command his teacher, the Bible, from Genesis to Revelation, records as the will of God?

The history of the world cannot present a more stupid, self-stultifying specimen of dereliction of principle than this. The teacher demands emphatically in every page that the law of the Sabbath be observed every week, by all recognizing it as "the only infallible teacher," whilst the disciples of that teacher have not once for over three hundred years observed the divine precept! That immense concourse of Biblical Christians, the Methodists, have declared that the Sabbath has never been abrogated, whilst the followers of the Church of England, together with her daughter, the Episcopal Church of the United States, are committed by the twentieth article of religion, already quoted, to the ordinance that the Church cannot lawfully ordain anything *"contrary to God's written word."* God's written word enjoins His worship to be observed on *Saturday* absolutely, repeatedly, and most emphatically, with a most positive threat of death to him who disobeys. All the Biblical sects occupy the same self-stultifying position which no explanation can modify, much less justify.

How truly do the words of the Holy Spirit apply to this deplorable situation! *"Iniquitas mentita est sibi"* — "Iniquity hath lied to itself." Proposing to follow *the Bible only* as teacher, yet before the world, *the sole teacher* is ignominiously thrust aside, and the teaching and practice of the Catholic Church — "the mother of abominations," when it suits their purpose so to designate her — adopted, despite the most terrible threats pronounced by God Himself against those who disobey the command, "Remember to keep holy the Sabbath."

Before closing this series of articles, we beg to call the attention of our readers once more to our caption, introductory of each; viz., 1. The Christian Sabbath, the genuine offspring of the union of the Holy Spirit with the Catholic Church, His spouse. 2. The claim of Protestantism to any part therein proved to be groundless, self-contradictory, and suicidal.

The first proposition needs little proof. The Catholic Church for over one thousand years before the existence of a Protestant, by virtue of her divine mission, changed the day from Saturday to Sunday. We say by virtue of her divine mission, because He who called Himself the "Lord of the Sabbath," endowed her with His own power to teach, "He that heareth you, heareth Me;" commanded all who believe in Him to hear her, under penalty of being placed with the "heathen and publican;" and promised to be with her to the end of the world. She holds her charter as the teacher from Him — a charter as infallible as perpetual. The Protestant world at its birth found the Christian Sabbath too strongly entrenched to run counter to its existence; it was therefore placed under the necessity of acquiescing in the arrangement, thus implying the Church's right to change the day, for over three hundred years. The Christian Sabbath is therefore *to this day*, the acknowledged offspring of the Catholic Church as spouse of the Holy Ghost, without a word of remonstrance from the Protestant world.

Let us now, however, take a glance at our second proposition, with the *Bible alone* as the teacher and guide in faith and morals. This teacher *most emphatically forbids any change in the day for paramount reasons*. The command calls for a *"perpetual covenant."* The day commanded to be kept by the teacher *has never once been kept*, thereby developing an apostasy from an assumedly fixed principle, as self-contradictory, self-stultifying, and consequently as suicidal as it is within the power of language to express.

Nor are the limits of demoralization yet reached. Far from it. *Their pretense* for leaving the bosom of the Catholic Church was for apostasy from the truth *as taught in the written word*.

They adopted the written word as their sole teacher, which they had no sooner done than they abandoned it promptly, as these articles have abundantly proved; and by a perversity as willful as erroneous, they accept the teaching of the Catholic Church in direct opposition to the plain, unvaried, and constant teaching of their sole teacher in the most essential doctrine of their religion, thereby emphasizing the situation in what may be aptly designated "a mockery, a delusion, and a snare."

> [**Editor's note** — It was upon this very point that the Reformation was condemned by the Council of Trent. The Reformers had constantly charged, as here stated, that the Catholic Church had apostatized from the truth *as contained in the written word*. "The written word," "The Bible and the Bible only," "Thus saith the Lord," these were their constant watchwords; and "The Scripture, as in the written word, the sole standard of appeal," this was the proclaimed platform of the Reformation and of Protestantism. "The Scripture *and tradition*," "the Bible as interpreted by the Church and according to the unanimous consent of the Fathers," this was the position and claim of the Catholic Church. This was the main issue in the Council of Trent, which was called especially to consider the questions that had been raised and forced upon the attention of Europe by the Reformers. The very first question concerning faith that was considered by the council was the question involved in this issue. There was a strong party even of the Catholics within the council who were in favor of abandoning tradition and adopting *the Scripture only*, as the standard of authority. This view was so decidedly held in the debates in the council that the pope's legates actually wrote to him that there was "a strong tendency to set aside tradition altogether and to make Scripture the sole standard of appeal." But to do this would manifestly be to go a long way toward justifying the claims of the Protestants. By this crisis there was devolved upon the ultra-Catholic portion of the council the task of convincing the others that "Scripture and *tradition*" was the only sure ground to stand upon. If this could be done, the council could be carried to issue a decree condemning the Reformation, otherwise not. The question was debated day after day, until the council was fairly brought to a standstill. Finally, after a long and intense mental strain,

the Archbishop of Reggio came into the council with substantially the following argument to the party who held for Scripture alone: —

"The Protestants claim to stand upon the written word only. They profess to hold the Scripture alone as the standard of faith. They justify their revolt by the plea that the Church has apostatized from the written word and follows tradition. Now the Protestants' claim, that they stand upon the written word only, is not true. Their profession of holding the Scripture alone as the standard of faith, is false. PROOF: The written word explicitly enjoins the observance of the seventh day as the Sabbath. They do not observe the seventh day, but reject it. If they do truly hold the Scripture alone as their standard, they would be observing the seventh day as is enjoined in the Scripture throughout. Yet they not only reject the observance of the Sabbath enjoined in the written word, but they have adopted and do practice the observance of Sunday, for which they have only the tradition of the Church. Consequently the claim of 'Scripture alone as the standard,' *fails;* and the doctrine of 'Scripture *and tradition*' as essential, is fully established, the Protestants themselves being judges."

There was no getting around this, for the Protestants' own statement of faith — the Augsburg Confession, 1530 — had clearly admitted that "the observation of the Lord's day" had been appointed by "the Church" only.

The argument was hailed in the council as of Inspiration only; the party for "Scripture alone," surrendered; and the council at once unanimously condemned Protestantism and the whole Reformation as only an unwarranted revolt from the communion and authority of the Catholic Church; and proceeded, April 8, 1546, "to the promulgation of two decrees, the first of which enacts, under anathema, that Scripture *and tradition* are to be received and venerated equally, and that the deutero-canonical [the apocryphal] books are part of the canon of Scripture. The second decree declares the Vulgate to be the sole authentic and standard Latin version, and gives it such authority as to supersede the original texts; forbids the interpretation of Scripture contrary to the sense received by the Church, 'or even contrary to the unanimous consent of the Fathers,'" etc.[1]

Thus, it was the inconsistency of the Protestant practice with the Protestant profession that gave to the Catholic Church her long-sought and anxiously desired ground upon which to condemn Protestantism and the whole Reformation movement as only a selfishly ambitious rebellion against church authority. And in this vital controversy the key, the chiefest and culminative expression, of the Protestant inconsistency, was in the rejection of the Sabbath of the Lord, the seventh day, enjoined in the Scriptures, and the adoption and observance of the Sunday as enjoined by the Catholic Church.

And this is today the position of the respective parties to this controversy. Today, as this document shows, this is the vital issue upon which the Catholic Church arraigns Protestantism, and upon which she condemns the course of popular Protestantism as being "indefensible, self-contradictory, and suicidal." What will these Protestants, what will this Protestantism, do? — **Editor.**]

Should any of the reverend parsons, who are habituated to howl so vociferously over every real or assumed desecration of that pious fraud, the *Bible Sabbath*, think well of entering a protest against our logical and Scriptural dissection of their mongrel pet, we can promise them that any reasonable attempt on their part to gather up the *disjecta membra* of the hybrid, and to restore to it a galvanized existence, will be met with genuine cordiality and respectful consideration on our part.

But we can assure our readers that we know these reverend howlers too well to expect a solitary bark from them in this instance. And they know us too well to subject themselves to the mortification which a further dissection of this antiscriptural question would necessarily entail. Their policy now is to "lay low," and they are sure to adopt it.

---

[1] See the proceedings of the Council; Augsburg Confession; and Encyclopedia Britannica, article "Trent, Council of."

APPENDIX 1

THESE articles are reprinted, and this leaflet is sent forth by the publishers, because it gives from an undeniable source and in no uncertain tone, the latest phase of the Sunday-observance controversy, which is now, and which indeed for some time has been, not only a national question with the leading nations, but also an international question. Not that we are glad to have it so; we would that it were far otherwise. We would that Protestants everywhere were so thoroughly consistent in profession and practice that there could be no possible room for the relations between them and Rome ever to take the shape which they have now taken.

But the situation in this matter is now as it is herein set forth. There is no escaping this fact. It therefore becomes the duty of the International Religious Liberty Association to make known as widely as possible the true phase of this great question as it now stands. Not because we are pleased to have it so, but because it is so, whatever we or anybody else would or would not be pleased to have.

It is true that we have been looking for years for this question to assume precisely the attitude which it has now assumed, and which is so plainly set forth in this leaflet. We have told the people repeatedly, and Protestants especially, and yet more especially have we told those who were advocating Sunday laws and the recognition and legal establishment of Sunday by the United States, that in the course that was being pursued they were playing directly into the hands of Rome, and that as certainly as they succeeded, they would inevitably be called upon by Rome, and Rome in possession of power too, to render to her an account as to why Sunday should be kept. This, we have told the people for years, would surely come. And now that it *has* come, it is only our duty to make it known as widely as it lies in our power to do.

It may be asked, Why did not Rome come out as boldly as this before? Why did she wait so long? It was not for her interest to do so before. When she should move, she desired to move with power, and power as yet she did not have. But in their strenuous efforts for the national, governmental recognition and establishment of Sunday, the Protestants of the United States were doing more for her than she could possibly do for herself in the way of getting governmental power in her hands. This she well knew, and therefore only waited. And now that the Protestants, in alliance with her, have accomplished this awful thing, she at once rises up in all her native arrogance and old-time spirit, and calls upon the Protestants to answer to her for their observance of Sunday. This, too, she does because she is secure in the power which the "Protestants" have so blindly placed in her hands. In other words, the power which the "Protestants" have thus put into her hands she will now use to their destruction. Is any other evidence needed to show that the *Catholic Mirror* (which means the Cardinal and the Catholic Church in America) has been waiting for this, than that furnished on page 27 of this leaflet? Please turn back and look at that page, and see that quotation clipped from the New York *Herald* in 1874, and which is now brought forth thus. Does not this show plainly that that statement of the Methodist bishops, the *Mirror*, all these nineteen years, has been keeping for just such a time as this? And more than this, the "Protestants" will find more such things which have been so laid up, and which will yet be used in a way that will both surprise and confound them.

This at present is a controversy between the Catholic Church and Protestants. As such only do we reproduce these editorials of the *Catholic Mirror*. The points controverted are points which are claimed by "Protestants" as in their favor. The argument is made by the Catholic Church; the answer devolves upon those Protestants who observe Sunday, not upon us. We can truly say, "This is none of our funeral." If they do not answer, she will make their silence their confession that she is right, and will act toward them accordingly. If they do answer, she will use against them their own words, and as occasion may demand, the power which they have put into her hands. So that, so far as she is concerned, whether the "Protestants" answer or not, it is all the same. And how she looks upon them, and the spirit in which she proposes to deal with them henceforth is clearly manifested in the challenge made in the last paragraph of the reprint articles.

There is just one refuge left for the Protestants. That is to take their stand squarely and fully upon "the written word only," "the Bible and the Bible alone," and thus upon the Sabbath of the Lord. Thus acknowledging no authority but God's, wearing no sign but His (Ezekiel 20:12, 20), obeying His command, and shielded by His power, they shall have the victory over Rome and all her alliances, and stand upon the sea of glass, bearing the harps of God, with which their triumph shall be forever celebrated. (Revelation 18, and 15:2-4.)

It is not yet too late for Protestants to redeem themselves. Will they do it? Will they stand consistently upon the Protestant profession? or will they still continue to occupy the "indefensible, self-contradictory, and suicidal position of professing to be Protestants, yet standing on Catholic ground, receiving Catholic insult, and bearing Catholic condemnation? Will they indeed take the written word only, the Scripture alone, as their sole authority and their sole standard? or will they still hold the "indefensible, self-contradictory, and suicidal" doctrine and practice of following the authority of the Catholic Church and of wearing the sign of her authority? Will they keep the Sabbath of the Lord, the seventh day, according to Scripture? or will they keep the Sunday according to the tradition of the Catholic Church?

Dear reader, which will *you* do?

Appendix 2

Since the first edition of this publication was printed, the following appeared in an editorial in the *Catholic Mirror* of December 23, 1893:

"The avidity with which these editorials have been sought, and the appearance of a reprint of them by the International Religious Liberty Association, published in Chicago, entitled, 'Rome's Challenge: Why Do Protestants Keep Sunday?' and offered for sale in Chicago, New York, California, Tennessee, London, Australia, Cape Town, Africa, and Ontario, Canada, together with the continuous demand, have prompted the *Mirror* to give permanent form to them, and thus comply with the demand.

"The pages of this brochure unfold to the reader one of the most glaringly conceivable contradictions existing between the practice and theory of the Protestant world, and unsusceptible of any rational solution; the theory claiming the Bible alone as the teacher, which unequivocally and most positively commands Saturday to be kept 'holy,' whilst their practice proves that they utterly ignore the unequivocal requirements of their teacher, the Bible, and occupying Catholic ground for three centuries and a half, by the abandonment of their theory, they stand before the world today the representatives of a system the most indefensible, self-contradictory, and suicidal that can be imagined.

"We feel that we cannot interest our readers more than to produce the 'Appendix'[1] which the International Religious Liberty Association, an

---

[1] At the close of this editorial, Appendix I of this pamphlet was reprinted in full — Editor.

ultra-Protestant organization, has added to the reprint of our articles. The perusal of the Appendix will confirm the fact that our argument is unanswerable, and that the only resource left the Protestants is either to retire from Catholic territory where they have been squatting for three centuries and a half, and accepting their own teacher, the Bible, in good faith, as so clearly suggested by the writer of the 'Appendix,' commence forthwith to keep the Saturday, the day enjoined by the Bible from Genesis to Revelation; or, abandoning the Bible as their sole teacher, cease to be squatters, and a living contradiction of their own principles, and taking out letters of adoption as citizens of the kingdom of Christ on earth — His Church — be no longer victims of self-delusive and necessary self-contradiction.

"The arguments contained in this pamphlet are firmly grounded on the word of God, and having been closely studied with the Bible in hand, leave no escape for the conscientious Protestant except the abandonment of Sunday worship and the return to Saturday, commanded by their teacher, the Bible, or, unwilling to abandon the tradition of the Catholic Church, which enjoins the keeping of Sunday, and which they have accepted in direct opposition to their teacher, the Bible, consistently accept her in all her teachings. Reason and common sense demand the acceptance of one or the other of these alternatives: either Protestantism and the keeping holy of Saturday, or Catholicity and the keeping of Sunday. Compromise is impossible."

Appendix 2

Adventist Pioneer Library

For more information, visit:
www.APLib.org

or write to:
apl@netbox.com

Made in the USA
Columbia, SC
14 March 2024